THE WATER CARRIER

❖

by

Steve Straight

CURBSTONE PRESS

FIRST EDITION, 2002
Reprinted 2004.
Copyright © 2002
All Rights Reserved

Printed on acid-free paper by BookMobile
Cover design: Mark Bilokur
Photograph (front cover): "14 May 90_01" © Chuck Doswell,
Outdoor Images, Inc.

This book was published with the support of
the Connecticut Commission on the Arts and
donations from many individuals. We are very
grateful for this support.

Library of Congress Cataloging-in-Publication Data

Straight, Steve, 1954-
    Water carrier / by Steve Straight.-- 1st ed.
        p. cm.
    ISBN 1-880684-83-7 (pbk. : alk. paper)
    1. New England--Poetry. 2. City and town life--Poetry.   I. Title.

    PS3619.T73 W38 2002
    811'.6--dc21   2001005930

Published by
CURBSTONE PRESS   321 Jackson St.   Willimantic, CT 06226
info@curbstone.org • www.curbstone.org

ACKNOWLEDGMENTS:

Grateful acknowledgment is made to the editors of the following journals where some of these poems, some in other forms, first appeared:

The Blue Guitar: "The Tail," "What Teachers Dream"; *Breakthrough News:* "Touch"; *Common Ground Review:* "Lesson," "Littering," "While Sorting Books"; *Compost:* "Harvest"; *Connecticut Review:* "Encounter in June," "The Water Carrier," "What Teachers Dream"; *Freshwater:* "The Art of Dreaming," "Bird Stories," "Last Summer," "Leftovers"; *UConn Traditions:* "I Learn to Accept a Certain Amount of Melancholy."

Special thanks to the many friends who have supported this work, to Martín Espada, Vivian Shipley, Mike DiRaimo, Edwina Trentham, Ed Diemente, Julie and Nick Stone (for my own Yaddo), Christina Pham, and my students, especially Kate Foran and Hank Gromelski. My deepest gratitude goes to Rennie McQuilkin for his honest counsel and generous spirit.

This book is dedicated to my wife
and first reader,
Marian Maccarone.

Contents

THE WATER CARRIER

1.

The Water Carrier

Lugging the forty-eight-pound Poland Spring water jug
up from the cellar, it strikes me how much of my life
is spent transporting water. How many gallons of it
carried to the garden, to the flower beds, to bushes
and trees, lately with blue grains of fertilizer
dissolved in it, trip after trip to the linden tree, trying
to restore its vigor. How many pots of pasta water
lifted from stove to sink, how many cups of lemon tea
delivered to my wife over twenty-five hundred days of
marriage.

My wife, an Aquarian, reminds me that nothing compares
to the out and out hauling by women and other slaves
over the centuries, for cooking, washing, bathing,
slopping, drinking. Tons of it per person per life,
a life stooped and shortened by it. I see films
of people yoked between pails of it and feel sorry
when it spills over the sides in the normal rhythm
of walking, all that spilled having to be carried again.

The Buddhists tell us it all comes down to that
and chopping wood. Carry it only to carry it,
mindful of the watering can handle's convexness
and smoothness, the way the Poland Spring jug
hugs my chest, the lemon and honey steam
rising from the tea. No mistake.

Seventy-five percent of us is liquid, of course,
in that perfect proportion we share with the Earth
and the water it carries through space. I log the miles
with it every day, have cameled it across the Mojave
in an air-conditioned Dodge, kayaked it down a stretch

of the Connecticut, carried more than my share of it
soaked to the bone in the Burren, in County Clare,
wondering why the Earth needed it moved a few more miles
in my hat and hair, my shirt, pants, and shoes.

I've spent sick days, too, moving it only from
the hot side of the bed to the cool one, sweating,
and reminding myself of the funny dictum to force fluids,
my favorite by far the homemade orangeade
my mother brought me during bouts of tonsillitis.
Most days I slake my important thirst at water coolers
in hallways, or from the big glass pitcher of sun tea
my wife has squeezed a lemon into, whenever
my internal dipstick reads "add."

And what about the thickets behind left fields,
the edges of woods along highways, the sides of trees
and railroad tracks in moonlight where I have left it,
lightened my load, as they say. That I was meant to deliver it
then and there is yet another argument for design. And
although I can't transport it like the albatross over
thousands of miles of ocean, or the great thunderclouds
bowling overhead, sucking it from the earth and racing it
across vast expanses of sky, I am one of the many small
but efficient vessels on the planet, respirators. Even
now in my next exhalation I send some vapor forth,
on its way to become the next cloud.

2.

Haiku for Manchester

*"In pointillism, primary-color dots
are used to generate secondary colors."*

A town made of silk—
trees shimmer
in the moonlight.

In the old mill apartment,
a woman pours tea in a room
where a man once lost his thumb.

In Marlow's five and dime
a woman rubs the dust off a darning egg,
finds a price from 1964.

At the old State Theater,
with balcony and velvet curtain,
Jesus saves where John Wayne did.

Eight-bar blues
at the Hungry Tiger—
cold draft from the door.

Summer night at Charter Oak Park,
they pay with quarters
for basketball light.

Town boy's name
on the black Vietnam wall;
I remember his fearless jump shot.

After the great ice storm
branches encased in ice
rattle in the wind.

Someone dumped goldfish
in Center Springs pond—
now they're big enough to eat.

Hurricane winds lash the town pharmacy;
flattened men wait in a row
for the Daily Racing Form.

Stop and Shop bagger fresh from India
stares at the pumpkin in her hands
and smiles.

The harried cashier
punches unrequested lotto numbers—
good luck or bad?

Colored plastic bags stuck to tree branches—
not women's hats,
as I first saw them.

On top of the Route 84 light post,
a red-tailed hawk stares—
which car is small enough to eat?

After spring showers
at the mall,
cars leaking rainbows.

In the lot, wildflowers push through
island soil in a vast black sea—
how did they find it?

Inside the mall, stacks of toys
fifteen feet high—
the boy picks his nose.

The dinosaur bones—
ground to powder
for a home improvement store.

Cool summer morning—
the red fox pauses
near the abandoned coop.

Near new satellites of the mall—
wild turkeys cross the cold street
before dawn.

The Cape Cod House

Thirty years later I remember the names
up and down our street because few came or went,
jobs back then being promises kept: Blasko, Charest,
Rook, Hare, LeBlanc, Spicer, Hires, Gechas, Firnstahl.

I knew a neighbor's house before I went in
through the kitchen off the left-side driveway:
table to the right, sink and cupboards left, through
the doorway to the center hall, dining room to the right
then bathroom centered at the back, master bedroom
at the end of the hall, then into the living room, 10 by 15—
even in a Cape I'd never seen, I could predict where the sofa
would be, which cabinet held the Monopoly and Scrabble.

It was a Swiss Army knife of a house: the square space
behind the back stoop fit exactly one quarter cord of firewood,
neatly stacked; a rubber ball thrown at the side of the stoop
came back a grounder, if it hit the driveway first, a pop-up;
a chin-up bar sprung in the doorway between the kitchen
and hall passed for a gym; under the cellar hatchway the steps
became a second refrigerator for the turkey carcass in its huge
speckled pan; boxes of ornaments and lights came down
from the eaves behind my sister's bed two weeks before Christmas
to the rearranged living room, and before New Year's
my father would shuffle it all back, matching chair legs
with the dents in the rug.

In all our houses the kids' domain was the cellar,
shared with its workbench and indoor clothesline
and set tubs and furnace, but big enough maybe
for a ratty old couch and a radio, and a ping pong table
with a tight wall on one side and a blue pillow

taped to the elbow of the water pipe so the tallest boy
wouldn't crack his head open lunging for the ball.

In large families the Cape was more like an ark
with kids separated only by gender, two or three
to an upstairs room, dreaming of privacy but growing up
like citizens, learning to fight and share and clean up the mess.

When I was thirteen I tasted the future of housing,
going to John Rubinow's house, Doc Rubinow's son,
on the other side of town, to watch the All-Star game
on a color TV. The TV had its own room, with paneled walls
and new furniture and something called a coffee table with
glass bowls of M & Ms and Good 'n' Plenty on its glass top.
I understood that people only went in this room to watch
television. The house had other rooms for doing only one
thing, and walk-in closets, and a three-car garage. Of course
when I came home our Cape looked small, but somehow
we all fit inside, somehow it kept us dry.

At the Mill

—Lydall and Foulds, 1973

Anna hunched over a pile of cardboard slabs,
feeding them into a hundred-foot machine that
sheared off the ragged edges and sliced them
in half; her right hand, gloved in black, shoved
each board into spinning rollers at the precise
instant the end of the previous board disappeared,
her left hand feeling the next one's corner.
Board after board she hit the spot,
keeping her head sunk to an angle where
she gauged the slide of boards almost through
her eyebrow. For twenty minutes I studied
this production of magic until I was to relieve
her. She stepped off the platform, still bent
and holding her back, mumbled something
in Polish and smiled, waving me on as two
men wheeled in the next stack. I tried to copy
her angle and method, glancing over to see
her nod, sipping from her brown mug of coffee,
and soon understood she was stooped for life.

In the washroom I met Frank, who spent ten
hours a day dying paper pulp he swirled with
a long pole in a vat of steaming blue dye. Now
he stood at the circular sink, his foot on the rail
that made water flow in thin rivulets, like some
town fountain. He wore overalls, but every
exposed piece of skin was blue. As I stared he
attacked his skin with yellow soap the consistency
of sand, rubbing the grit into his pores and then
scraping the light blue film with his fingernails.

He looked at me out of bright eyes, rinsing off
the first coat, and then continued.

I don't know why they hired me, at nineteen,
moving one step up from bagging groceries,
unless I looked that desperate, because this was
the deal at Lydall and Foulds:

> You get to America any way you can and
> we'll give you a job and you can bring
> your family one by one and learn to pledge
> allegiance, and all day long you can speak
> your Polish to anyone but the foreman,
> and there'll be a union, but when the
> contract comes up we'll take care of it
> and anything else here you don't see.

So they called me American Boy, and since I
hadn't worked tobacco like my friends who
came home each summer afternoon exhausted
and stinking of it, this was my first look at
the very gears inside the engine.

Many days I worked opposite Stanley, 55,
who stood at the other end of a table beside
the roaring dryer, ready to lift his end of the
soggy blue slab onto the ever-clanking
conveyor belt as soon as I dug my fingers under
the corners; we slapped the twenty-pound board
onto the belt within two inches of the last one,
now cranking into the mouth of the giant machine,
then lifted the sheet of silk that separated boards
and slung it over a horse. That was it, over and over.
Two and a half hours later Stan, over six feet tall
but gaunt, his face the grey of the cinder block

walls, took his twenty-minute lunch at the table
by the machine; his eyes fixed on the motion
of his relief man, he raised his bologna sandwich
evenly to his mouth as if guided by a system
of pulleys, bit delicately one small portion of it,
and lowered it to the table in the same speed,
at the same arc. He slid his thin card into the
punchclock and took his vacant place again.

We were drying the boards that Frank had dyed
and which the men at the end of the dryer
would weigh and stack and which Anna would
trim and which the men and women sitting on stools
at the feet of Anna's machine would inspect and
count as it spit them out every three and a half
seconds, cuts appearing up and down the forearms
they used to protect their eyes and cheeks, serving
the machines that never stopped as we passed
the baton of pain.

The truth is, I never knew their names, or
wouldn't remember them, ground into the
drone of all thoughts the mind could produce
in such a place, just as none of us knew what we
made. Cardboard, yes, but for what? I heard
it became the insides of doors or the soles of shoes
but for all we knew each day's stacks on pallets
might be shipped around the block to become
the next day's pulp.

Hobby

First, that he is reaching into
a garbage can, into the coffee grounds
and fruit peels and wet McDonald's scum
for a discarded soda can worth five cents.
He bags them one at a time.

Second, that he is an old man
with a khaki jacket and neat cap
and a pipe in his mouth. He could be
baiting a hook for his grandson or
bending to pick a beetle off his roses.

Third, that he is a crow finding
a bun corner left in the rain, or a dead
squirrel with eye unplucked. He sorts
our detritus with the patience we didn't have,
redeeming what can be. As he moves on
to the next receptacle, adjusting his pipe and
shaking his giant plastic maraca to settle the cans,
I think I hear him hum.

At Spike's Garage

At Spike's Garage near the university
I pull in for gas. It's the olden days,
and Ernie the mechanic comes out
from the bay to pump my gas.

I'm in grad school and my second year
teaching freshman English, and Ernie's
fixed my car a few times at his house
to spare me Spike's cut for parts and labor.

Ernie, a townie, about 22, bushy haired
with greasy blue coveralls, oil under
his nails, locks the pump on and says,
"So, professor, what're ya teachin'?"

It's Friday, and I remember the dazed group
I tried to teach that morning, sleepy and
hung over, leading a discussion just one more
session pulling teeth. "Hamlet,"
I tell him. "You know, Shakespeare."

He stops in mid-squeegee as blue water
streams down my window. "Hamlet!"
he spits. "Ugh. I had to read that in
high school. It was awful, so boring."

He seems to say what my students only
thought, and for a second I wonder if
I'm cut out for this, trying to teach great
works to people who hate them.

"Hamlet!" he says again, shaking
the squeegee. "He didn't even know
when to shit." Finally he pulls it across
the window, wiping the excess liquid off
the rubber with his fingers. "Macbeth,"
he says. "Now *that* was a play."

Green Card

Once there was a jumpshot
that didn't go in
in a big game
that rolled around
and out

and the small black guard
with steel spring legs
sank to the floor
without his degree

to the pet store
in his hometown
tending the fish
that nose the glass
in small green tanks.

Once there was a jumpshot
that wouldn't go in
at the big white college

that fanned his dream
burning since childhood
of baselines painted gold

and the small black man
sank to the floor
of America.

No blood, no foul.

How They Got Here

—for my students

Rich carried his high school diploma to the local
bank in 1975 and learned job after job, treated
everyone he met with respect and humility and
rose to the corner office with the desk, two chairs,
and tall ficus plant, his two sons in college. After
the bank was swallowed, and swallowed again,
the new boss took the train straight from Yale,
spent the year convincing him that bad spelling
and plain words would number his days, and all
his confidence slid through a trap door down
a long, dark shaft.

Michelle emerged from the fog of neglect and doubt
that her family had pumped into her room for years.
Thirty, with a small child, unemployed and still
chained to her father's house, she walked three
miles here each day, swapping shoulders with
her load of books every few steps and dreaming
of the day when one of the directions would not
be uphill.

Masako sat quietly in the back of the room, sitting
up straight to peer over the tall grass of Japanese
that surrounded her. Weeded out of the college
track back in Japan, she became housewife for an
engineer whose company sent him abroad. Now
in the new world everyone spoke so fast, and even
her quick fingers riffling through the two-way
dictionary could find no trace of the idioms and
clipped words that peppered her professor's
sentences.

Hank was a runner. Each day his Indian legs
pushed up the Wickham Park hills or his feet
slapped the cinder track as he tried to keep a step
ahead of the neighbor's dog, his brothers' fists,
his mother's tears. About the time his knees
gave out and everything caught him at once,
the local trade school coughed him out with
the other misfits and outlaws, more than a
few with talent collecting under their fingernails.

Butch walks the jungle path every day, a morning
mist rising as he fingers the trigger of his M-16,
the metal like part of his arm. He's on point, has
circled around to where the enemy should be, and
with each short breath the hairs in his nose work
like antennas. Suddenly a figure jumps out from
the brush a short way off, and before he can
recognize the voice or face, it's the boy he practically
adopted from the village, who taught him trust
when he had none, dead at his feet, the gun
hot in his hand. Now, his brain has decided it's
time to get it all down.

Kate lay on the hard cot of chronic fatigue
for the last two years of high school, the thin
mattress absorbing her tears and sweat, hour
after hour watching her breath and imagining
her hands and feet heavy and warm until they
were. As a last resort, her father found a magician
in New Jersey with spells of peroxide drip, new
medicines, and pink vials of vitamin shots
she could taste within minutes, until one day,
from the nightmare no one understood, she awoke.

Kendall, pegged in third grade as "mischievous,"
by ninth grade "dangerous," whose father thought
the Army would help him pay attention, who
washed out of basic and washed up here, drums
all his fingers on the desk as the papers are handed
back, frowns at the comments littering the margins,
then looks up surprised when his professor
tells him he has a lot to say.

Freewrite

Write quickly, without stopping, for a measured time.
Don't worry about grammar, punctuation, or spelling.

Where I been is this, One day I'm down at the sight and the foreman says Jack, pick up those sheets of wallboard, I didn't even have my coffee yet. On the forth one I bend over like usual and its stuck on something. I give it a yank and what gives is my back, I can't even straighten up. It's like someone shot me in the spine with a nailgun, I tell the foreman and he says Jack, suck it up, but I don't give a shit and tell him so. Then I see his face change and he helps me to a stack of cinder blocks, Two operations later here I am for a new career. I'm not sure what yet, just something better than Would you like fries with that? or chasing stock at Wall Mart, No bennies, no union and oops we're leavin town next week. Where I'm goin don't have to be grand, like what you see on Tee Vee, just a couple rooms, a wife that loves me, and health for my kids. Maybe save enough to handle the next curveball. I don't blame the foreman, would of been worse ten years from now. The classroom's warm, the girls smell nice, and right now I'll just keep takin life with a grain of sand.

At the Exam, Reading

—for Richard Russo

As I lift my head from page seventy-four of the novel, I sense
the student to my right with bleary eyes must have crashed on
her sister's couch after her parents kicked her out for staying
up all night with her boyfriend, even though she told them
they spent the night just talking in the front seat of his father's
Nissan.

When she turns to her neighbor during the exam and whispers
a few phrases before the neighbor smiles, I know they aren't
cheating, that they've bonded from my attacks on their prose,
that sharing this exam is the last gasp of being on the same
side of things, as the neighbor, whose writing has improved
and who may work her way into B territory with a deft exam,
is wearing tall suede boots, khaki pants, and a preppy sweater
that indicate her aspirations for a life beyond a raised ranch
and more bills than she can pay.

I fold the novel closed on the fingers of my right hand, feel the
smooth pages like a glove of language, and sigh. A third
student, bearing down hard on the page with her ballpoint
pen, her head cocked at a sharp angle and tongue jutting from
pursed lips, reminds me of a girl I knew in the third grade.
This student now, though remarkably beautiful at 20 or 21,
strains with the force of her pen to impress her third-grade
teacher, as if neatness still counts and dark letters have more
meaning.

An A student comes forward to hand in her exam, early, and
nods her thanks for my thorough critiques all semester, and I
know from the tilt of this nod that she is closer to finding the

confidence to be openly bright, to say what she thinks without being prodded, that it means the boyfriend she's spoken of and who's majoring in accounting while working for the school newspaper and who will one day be a model citizen, indeed the mayor of this town, is history.

I glance out the window at what remains of the snow that fell three days ago, and the evergreens with the oak leaves clotted beneath them don't belong to my world, exactly, but remain between whatever the truth of this day may be and the certain images of the world against my fingertips.

What Teachers Dream

It is an old classroom, with a smoky transom
tilted above the door, high walls stained brown
and two-person wood tables bolted to the floor.
Of course he has never taught physics before,
nor taken it, but he can't remember that,
can only feel the swollen sense of being unprepared.

What is so sweet, though, is the way the students
hunch forward expectantly in their seats,
mechanical pencils in their hands like furled umbrellas
on the shore of knowledge, poised to absorb the nonsense
scrawled on the board. By the way the chalk dust
feels on his fingers, and by the way the 2's are formed
in the equation moored to the diagram, he can tell,
too, that despite the depth of his confusion
he is prepared to try.

The Great Path

—last day of spring classes at Manchester
Community College, sometime in the 21st century

That was the day Angelo raised his skinny hand at the back
    of the class and asked, "Could you give us a list of novels
    to read over the summer?" and ten other students
    nodded their heads.

That was the day Jahvonne brought her grandmother
    to math class to show her how cool parabolic curves
    were, splashed onto the forty-foot screen
    for the hushed crowd in the theater.

At lunch that day the madrigal choir waltzed through the caf
    in their blue velvet and silk, and the students,
    librarians and accountants mixed at noisy tables paused
    to join in parts on "Now Is the Month of Maying."

The applause wafted out to the biology students digging
    the college garden, old and young harvesting
    the organic arugula and peas and greens
    for the annual Spring Dinner that night.

After lunch that day students taught *their* final classes
    in raising kids and fixing old cars and growing
    fruit trees and making clothes, as rapt professors
    took pages of notes.

That afternoon out on the ballfield one of the deans
    shucked the donut off his bat and stepped
    to the plate for a few exhibition whacks.
    The star shortstop, a Truman scholar, leaned
    on the backstop signing autographs for awed kids
    as the crowd of 5,000 shifted happily in their sunny seats.

Before dinner many walked slowly up the long path
    to the Grove of the Spirits to pray and to meditate,
    or just to put their hands on the old trees and listen.

At the great dinner, the president wheeled her way through
    the crowd to the podium and opened with a good joke
    about the old days, when fellowship was replaced
    by meetings.

In the evening that day the New York critics arrived by train
    to scope the new art show, and students in the galleries
    and halls and courtyard stood by their oils and
    sculptures sorting their offers.

That was the day no one skipped a class, the day no one
    threatened a teacher or scared a student or snubbed
    a member of the staff, the day no one walked to her car
    in fear, the day no one anywhere stroked a remote
    control, the day no one trained for a corporate cell,
    the day no one dreaded a doctor's bill, the day no one
    died for someone's greed, the day nothing in the
    world died of neglect.

That was the day after the game and dinner and the opening
    and the new play that Luis the maintainer stopped
    cleaning by the library fireplace and signed his new
    novel for everyone long into the night.

3.

The Deepest Breath

I'm fifteen I'm naked I'm at the edge of the pool
and everything about me is small. Ross Pastel
has already done it, but he swims breaststroke on the swim team,
so 50 yards underwater means holding his breath for
only 30 seconds. Another boy has made it, but 23 of us
have not, and remember how small I am. The previous week
after a lap and a half failure I had walked to the short wall,
sat down, and then found myself a sack of numb limbs
on the floor being told to take it easy.

I'm fifteen I'm naked I'm at the edge of the pool
and everything about me is small, including my lungs.
To make it I'll have to hyperventilate, but Mr. Cobb
says we can't so I've snuck the breaths in, storing
secret molecules, as I sat on the wall with the other boys.
By the time my turn comes
I've got so much oxygen I'm smiling
and everybody must wonder about me.

I'm fifteen I'm naked and I'm off.
The water's cold jolts me and I have to fight
to stay calm, because excitement eats oxygen. But here
underwater I'm not as naked and glide a good
ten yards before my first stroke, then open my eyes
and begin. My stroke is focused and smooth: a solid kick
more like a sidestroke kick, then sweep my hands
out, back and glide. No strain. No sound. I am
a little fish all full of slippery purpose.

At the turn, at 25 yards, I feel good and glide back at least
five or six. I've done this each class all December, two
times a week to begin class, so I know the terrain of this

consciousness like my own house. It is my own very long room.
A glimpse of thought about air and I change the subject
quick, knowing it's way too early. I think of my father
diving off the dock when I was eight. I thought he'd never
come up, or couldn't imagine where. Months later I'd see
his head way off in the middle of the lake, it seemed.
I savor the remnant, the last vestige of that film at the lake
and squeak out a few more yards.

I'm fifteen I'm naked, dammit, and I hate Mr. Cobb
and it's one on one with my lungs now, with my brain,
which are the same thing now. I try to scare myself
with passing out again, this time underwater with
everyone rushing in to save my scrawny little
wart of a body but the pain in my brain
won't let me think of anything else.

                                    Go up, it says,
leering at me, or you'll die. You'll have to go now or you
won't even make it to the surface
but I'm fifteen I'm naked and for the first time
I can see the wall and I know in a flash that all along
I've been swimming to a naked place inside me,
that I'm swimming to God, that contained in
this breath is all I need to know.

Something About My Grandfather

—for Charles C. Chayer

Something about the blood grime from the guts of the worm
drying on my grandfather's fingers. Something about hearing
his breathing as he baited my hook, the long rasp of each
breath in his throat. Something about the sun glancing off
the lake and off his bald head, which I thought he might wax.
Something about the smell of the Evinrude as he adjusted
the choke for the second try, after a sigh. Something about
imagining the black Bible with red edges in his clean hands
the next day in church, the way he looked so comfortable
in his black robe. Something about the measured pace
with which he did everything. Something about the way
he spread the fourteen or fifteen playing cards out
across his fingers as we played Saratoga, a plump thumb
pinning them in place; the glee with which he turned over
the last red three.

More than once at dinner after church, when the whole family
gathered at the table extended by all three leaves, I would notice
under the buzz of conversation about new cousins or
congregation politics or the roast, my grandfather was silent.
He had paused with his forearms against the edge of the table,
his fingertips together to form an arch, and just stared ahead,
as if wondering how his life had spun down to exactly this.
But I would follow his gaze, if I could, trying to see where it
aimed, if it did. Then I would connect the gaze with what was
left on his plate.
"Grandfather," I'd say, "would you like some peas?"
"I'd love some," he'd say, the reverie ended.

Leftovers

Ten days later he's still eating the chicken legs
she cooked and left on the stove, which she told him
to refrigerate, one of the last things she said.
"Waste not, want not," he says.

He navigates the refrigerator with a combination
of thick lenses, finding containers of cottage cheese,
crushed pineapple, and raisins—all, he realizes,
from a sandwich she made, and makes one
for himself. The kitchen is so quiet he hears
his own mandible clicking, like a second hand
that stops when he does.

Of the items she bought and left on the counter
the day before going to the hospital, he has less idea.
For a man who never cooked, fresh garlic, balsamic
vinegar, and even pasta are more like souvenirs
than food. At sea now, he will learn, as he says,
first to boil water.

He enters the territory of her chair, her dark blue duchy
in the Florida Room. He finds bills and pays them,
though credit card computers, like respirators,
will keep her alive for months. In her address book
suddenly a Christmas card list—her friends
who won't have heard. So much of death
is notification, he thinks. Over and over
one must write or speak it.

The first of his sins to surface appears
in a pile of unfinished crossword puzzles
buried by her chair. He remembers his

harsh remark about how she couldn't finish them
anymore. That and the single tissue tucked
next to the cushion, a habit older than their children,
sink him into the chair for the first time in years.

Her medicines he sorts by usability and date,
knowing well that even old Demerol
is not trash, especially to a man with diverticulosis.
He plans to live six more years, he tells me,
to eighty-seven. He'll take most meals
at the hospital mess, driving roads he knows
and almost all right turns to reach it.

In their bedroom, her bed still has the fresh sheets
he had put on that last morning, Army tight.
On her bureau a still life of pocketbook, glasses, watch.
He is in no rush to scatter her ashes among
the palmettos and laurel oaks out back. For now,
there is time to open her closet again
and sink his nose into her dress.

Yesterday's

Away from home, and between visits
to my dying father, I order a meal
in a restaurant called Yesterday's,
a meal he would order, creamed
chipped beef on toast, an Army meal
called SOS that reminded him of Oahu.
My dad has aged ten years in the past
two months, his white hair now unruly wisps
that jut from his head like sails. He says
his words can't keep up with his thoughts,
and I tell him that's true for everyone.
The green beans, overcooked or from a can,
take me back to holding my father's hand
as we trudge up the snowy hill in Storrs
to the UConn basketball game when I am
five years old. The waitress asks if I'll have
dessert, says, "We have a delicious fried
cheesecake," and I say no, knowing that
tucked inside my father's coat pocket
will be candies of licorice and butterscotch.

Harvest

Giulia, age ten
and three quarters,
comes up from the garden
hugging a bounty of peppers
and tomatoes and squash
in her upturned skirt,
the catch so heavy she is doubled
over to contain it, her fingers pinching
the hem up near her chin, elbows
pressed to her sides like wings.

I see her hesitate
at the height of the counter,
wondering how she can empty the
tomatoes and peppers and squash from
her skirt without lifting it
so high.

I tell her
I will turn my back
so she can.

The Art of Dreaming

—for Catherine

Each night in preparation, she draws horses,
their long necks cooled by the deep shading
of her number one pencil,
nostrils dark, ears alert for commands.
She turns the leaves of art books, gathering a Parrish blue sky,
a stone tower from Edward Gorey, or water flowing uphill
in Escher's "Waterfall." She invites boys as well,
Seventeen hunks scissored free of their pages,
then snips her clothes off the glossy rack of J. Crew,
retraces the floor plan of the bedroom she designed
with the fireplace, stereo and walk-in spa. She slides a CD
into the player, and Tori Amos wails over and over
until a tune hums by itself in the background.
She'd like to slip easily from this world to the next,
but some nights a math problem knots itself
until thirty quick crunches release it,
or some girlfriend's snub
must be dissolved in warm tea.
When at last I hear the pull-chain recede
and the rustling of the sleeping bag cease, I can see
that night boat easing out from the dock of today.

While Sorting Books

—for Marian

Yesterday, as I finally alphabetized all the books
you and I brought to our marriage, stitching our lives
deeper together in the bookcase I built in, I found
a small journal from your other life.

As you told me, you started it after your first child
trapped you at home in a world before language,
back when your mate moved numbers for a living,
before the book club that saved you.

In it, a short list of vocabulary words, from
"*Smithsonian*, 1981"—*plethora, pundit, denizen,
diaspora, limned, fala*—each with a succinct phrase
following and all set down in neat script, as if
you couldn't bear losing them in the mist of duty.

In that list I heard the music of the syllable,
how words are shared like heirloom seeds,
and why I found eight dictionaries in the house,
including the pair of blue Webster's Sevenths
with the canvas rubbed off the corners, one per floor
in the home of our long conversation—
from *conversari*, to live, keep company with.

I Learn to Accept a Certain Amount
of Melancholy

Everyone does not swoon at light
glinting off a lake just after dawn
or swell at the skitterings of water striders
mottling the surface as if rain
fell from a clear blue sky.
This is strange to me.

You sidle into the day, unconvinced,
with a weight of previous days and years
stretching back before you were born,
in spite of yourself.

These forces sometimes clash.
One makes curtains just to draw them,
pulls a dark green sheet over her head
to keep the day at bay. One wakes always
before the alarm, is quick to leave a dream,
lifted by clouds that scud across the skylights.

From seeing your ways I see my own
and all our attempts
to contain what must overflow.

Touch

1.
You see me in the clearing, come up
behind and put your hand in mine.
Current surges through me, your touch
a sudden fire as if light had entered me.

2.
I find the zinnia's leaves quite wilted
though its orange face still gleams.
I pour water into the pot until
it's half an inch deep. As it seeps
into the soil, I speak to the plant,
apologize. Over the coursing of an hour
the message travels out to the leaves
who raise themselves level with the horizon.

3.
I shape our linden tree
by lopping off the lowest branches
with big snippers and a saw. The next day
sap has oozed to coat the wounds,
but it takes all week for the tree
to absorb these events, to sharpen
its perfect arrowhead against the sky
by sprouting new leaves.

4.
My boot stomps a shovel into the earth
at the base of the mountain. I am planting a tree.
Long after you have buried me,
when the tree turns light to shade,
the heart of the mountain will first sense
that pinprick of metal on its skin.

The Surprise

It was our fault for being early, back from Maine. At the door, for which Dave had our key, we heard scuffling inside, a racing from room to room. The lobsters squirmed slightly in the iced bag that hung from my hand. The fish market wasn't open on Sundays, we were ready to tell him, so we came home today.

As the door cracked open, first lipstick, then makeup, then a wig greeted us, followed by a blast of perfume that smelled like someone's aunt. The scuffle was over. There was only one person in the house, Dave, in a dress printed with blue flowers, with pearls dangling from his neck.

He stood by the stove, stammering, his hands conducting some unfinished fugue, occasionally looking down at his feet, at the red nails exposed in open-toe sandals, as if painted toenails were going too far, that everything else could be explained. In that moment the whole episode tottered on the brink of shame and remorse, but my wife simply said, "Dave, what a lovely dress," and the two began chattering like, well, girls.

I shuffled through the house with duffels and camping gear and leftover groceries, trip after trip, carrying smaller loads than I might. This was Dave, fellow grad student, baseball fan, friend, and now I knew nothing about him? Eventually I thought I might have to bring in the contents of the glove compartment or car cushions or the spare tire. Suddenly, though, I offered to cook the lobsters for all of us, insisting he stay for dinner, and Dave, after a pause in which he seemed to test both whether I meant it and whether he should like lobsters in his new life, said *yes*.

The Dead Battery

—for W.C.W.

Because the juice drained
out of the blue
Volvo's battery

and I had to curse, fool
with the yellow
jumper cables

I was still there
to catch the orange
tabby cat

trying to scoot past
with the squirming
chipmunk.

Encounter in June

Some days the year tries to drag me back
to the cold heart of February

and I lug the word cancer
wherever I go, cancer, which is not word
but weed, and chooses its own tense.

Some days it is that kind of spring.
But not today.

Today is a day for breathing,
for noticing rhythms too small to be noticed,
like the clattering of tiny toenails on plastic.
Today is this moment kneeling
at the end of a black downspout extension
with my hand held out on the ground, palm up,
breathing slowly and not moving an eyelash;
today is this moment appearing in the black tunnel
a chipmunk, quivering, nosing the great possibility
of faith, of taking the next step directly
into the human, onto the fingers, into the palm—
an island of skin surrounding a black pond of seeds.
Today is the shiny black eyes of the chippy
staring into mine, into the light at the end of the tunnel
that is me.

Bird Stories

I.

On a bleak day in late winter, rain, driving in a daze
something swooped in front of my windshield,
something big enough to suggest an alien world.

I pulled over, and though or because I had the flu,
was getting divorced, and all the defenses
I had ever known were down, I got out
and walked back to the spot in a soaking rain.

At first nothing—more bleakness in a ramshackle
house, a rusted car, an oak tree with dead leaves
that refused to detach themselves. Then, on a limb
about ten feet high, too far south, too tame, too white,
but there, unblinking, a snowy owl,
and the universe and I began to speak again.

II.

I had lit a woodstove long enough to take
a two-foot log through the door at the end.
I had turned the stovepipe damper open wide,
slid open the metal tongue below the door,
and air blew the flames in the chamber to a roar.
I began to turn toward the kitchen when I heard
a muffled thump against the damper.

Did I mention this was also a low day? Alone
but for my housemates' dogs in a farmhouse
with two-hundred-year-old creaks, a mood hung on me

like damp clothes. I had hoped the fire would get through
to that part of me that never wants to die. Now that sound
seemed to say, This is not just yesterday again.

As I turned back to the stove, a small bird
tumbled out of the lower opening onto the floor.
Stunned for a moment, it began to hop
across the room as I restrained the dogs. I opened
the front door and coaxed the bird—a purple finch, I think,
under the soot—gently with a straw broom, toward daylight.
It paused on the threshold as if it had centuries
and then flew right into the landscape.

The play has three acts, this reminded me, the game
has nine innings; in fact, you're batting for Wilson,
now get on in there and give the ball a whack.

III.

Our unsprayed yard and woods left wild
draw birds now by the dozens. Among them the catbird,
perched on the trellis top, flicking its long black
tuxedo tail at me, looking sharp in its sleek grey suit
as it glides to the garden fence, all chutzpah.

It's a borscht belt comic working up its catbird shtick,
swiping its beak on the sundial now, chortling
"Stop me if you heard this one," then cutting up
hecklers with its braying "mew, mew, mew," all the while
pivoting sharply to keep its keen black eye on the world.

Later, inside the blueberry netting, below the branches sagging
low with the plump berries we both love, a catbird
quick enough to enter the netting by some secret door

but not to find it again, thrashed itself to death
while we were away. No more high jinks,
no more gags, as I lifted the limp bird
and felt all the quickness drained out of it, only
enough presence to say, remember me,
remember how to live.

Ghost Suit

Three weeks before Christmas, my wife tells me
to close my eyes and stand up. I obey, and
in this vulnerable state she slips one sleeve
and then another up my arms and hoists
onto my shoulders the invisible jacket,
part of the ghost suit. When she takes it back,
murmuring about its perfection, I stand a few
extra moments in my darkness and imagine
that an alternate me is still wearing it, can
still feel its soft skin as it gets into the car
and drives off toward some kind of dinner
or reading where it will sip fine merlot and
accept compliments about its new jacket, and
I begin to wonder about the other selves
I've seen around the house, like the mirror
self I constantly assume is me.

When I screen a call and my answering machine
self comes on to ask people to deposit their
identities, that squeaky voice has little in common
with the voice I hear speaking to you now,
different still from the voice I hear when I speak
out loud, much more like the tinny voice
from the tiny tape recorder we played with
when I was ten, as if that voice never grew up.

Somehow the camera has never been a Cartesian
threat for me, except for the universal feeling
at motor vehicles that you've discovered
the grownup you were switched for at birth.
It's true, though, that we think of our ancestors
in old tintypes as mean, frozen people, not

people like us who had to hold an expression
for a strange box with a cape. Perhaps those tribes
had it right about the camera stealing their souls,
that the soul is a river not to be confused
with some point on the shore.

I can hardly think about the versions created
in the heads of each person I meet, or the dozens
of selves passing through each stranger who saw me
May 20th alone, walking down Broadway from
94th Street to Times Square wearing a blue
denim jacket and holding a black umbrella
against a light rain.

In junior high school, when classes changed
we swung around the halls in three or four lanes
each way. Afraid of being pegged as odd,
I always took the lane closest to oncoming traffic
and even in the rush of faces streaming
toward me could in a flash deliver a joke
or compliment tailored to each person I knew,
as if to demonstrate our connection by
reflecting some part of themselves.

My therapist has introduced me to a very insistent
fifteen-year-old she says I don't know well enough,
whom she has encouraged to write his own poems.
"Just drop into him," she says, smiling,
"and write from his point of view."
This, she says, is the road to integration,
a marvelous place where selves converse
and may even go on family vacations together
or have holidays without argument.

Whenever I come in from the outside world,
my cat, waking up, is never satisfied with merely
seeing me, must have the deeper identification
of smell as she sorts through the dozen or hundred
shades of me she detects on my fingers,
her nostrils working until she's got them all.
And if I offer first my forefinger and then my thumb,
she will smell each as if they are separate
creatures, capable of separate lives and experiences,
and if I look at them and press the two together,
in the which-feels-which I feel the small,
electric truth of that.

4.

Lesson

Standing by the side of the road in Jenner, California,
hitchhiking. At least that is the idea.
So few cars pass that one may not stop today.
It's sunny. Goats dispersed across the hillside behind me
chew their way up the green hill gradually, attentive.
The sea breeze carries phrases of seagull chatter
from below a cliff. In my pack are clothes, water,
oranges, three loaves of sourdough, peanuts, cheese.
Hung below the pack, a tent. I peel an orange,
tucking the continents of rind into a loose pocket.
Drops of juice fall onto the sand and on my boots.
A bee lands on the lip of a yellow blossom and walks
inside it. It emerges, dusted with pollen, drunk,
surprised by the generosity of light.

Cory Cove

—MacMahan Island, Maine

In early morning, the opposite of shadows:
streaks of light glint off the water onto the granite ledge
along the west side of the cove. A deer skirts the edge,

its sure feet compensating for a timid mind.
A lobsterman chugs into the mouth of the cove
and drops two pots, an orange buoy bobs in his wake,

and all about him seagulls buzz for chum. A heron
hunts in the shallows, lifting its feet like flippers.
In the binoculars I constantly reach for,

I spot an osprey in a fat nest atop a tall pine
on an island beyond the cove, six hundred yards away.
He sees me too, thinks, not fish, not fish.

Along the path a red squirrel pauses with its tail
over its head like a cowl, and I think of the winter
that must bury this place. Out from shore,

a tern stops in its current of air and hovers,
scanning the sea below. It must adjust
for the refraction of light, then dive through

the mirrors, trusting what it seeks will be there.

Captain Crunch

—MacMahan Island, Maine

Through strong binocs you spot
an orange boat working the cove,
captain at the wheel and his man
hauling the pots, two per orange buoy.
A dozen gulls flap white static
in the air, some lighting on bow
or stern, the men oblivious.

You never quite see a lobster
from this distance and wonder
if it feels to him like a carnival game
some days, like pop the balloon,
rigged against you with fifty grand
in the boat and traps, and debt
coming off two feelers at a time.

Just the same, that afternoon,
prompted by a single call
from the island, he chugs up
to the dock and stops on a dime,
doesn't even need to tie her off.
He's a big man with a face full
of dark black hair and an
honest smile with no top teeth.

He flips the lid of an old wooden box
and you stare into the maw
teeming with green-black bodies
climbing over each other.
Because you're green and

didn't know better, he empties
a plastic bag of bolts for you
and stuffs in four big ones,
minding you carry it home
with one hand under, so
you won't have to catch them
again with your hands.

Last Tack in Jewel

—for Julie and Nick Stone

"Ready about!"

Stationed at the starboard jib winch,
there's a moment to collect yourself again,
holding the fat dacron line softly in both hands.

You're the flesh and bone of his thoughts,
his commands more talking to himself
than anything else, and when you release
a line too soon, or your hand slips
on the winch handle, you know
without looking back that clouds cross his brow.

You'd like at least one perfect tack for him,
for yourself, for once to get all of it, the promise
of this big wind, yes, and to make something useful
of desire, and something more you can't name.

"Hard alec!"

Wait, now, wait, for the sails to luff
as the bow sweeps across the face of the wind.
Attach your muscles to the boat. Lock your foot
against the gunwale and pull, now, pull
for all you're worth. Expend yourself,
the faster now the less with the winch,
hand over hand till the line spirals out at your feet
and the boat begins to heel. When the slack is gone
just jam it in the cleat, lock in the winch handle
and if he says nothing you've done it clean.

With each crank around the boat heels more
until Adam the boat dog comes sliding down
the cockpit from the high port side. The cranking's
hard at this sharp tilt with the sea in your face
rushing over the gunwale, and it's hard to see
how a word like trimming could describe all this.
Just know you've done the job if sailing
past the same islands tomorrow
you don't recognize them.

"Lower the main!"

should be the command as you rock at the mooring
after the race. But that stiff wind has ripped the sail
right out of its loop at the tack corner, which he now
mends with a steel needle and thick thread
he found in some tin box below.

The mainsail wants more of this wind, though,
and snorts and bucks as if chomping a bit,
rattling the boom in its crutch and whipping
a free line through the air. It is addicted to it,
as you are, now, to the way the wind catches you
and makes you billow and stretch, and you wish
your life had windward marks to focus you
and clear your mind of the flotsam swirling
through it, and telltales to read
whenever you lost your course.

Hours later, standing in your kitchen,
you'll feel it through your feet and wonder
why you never noticed it before, the earth,
gently rocking in space.

Bobbing for Order

Beside me a woman
is reading and bobbing,
reading the Bible and bobbing.
She bobs her whole body,
leans into the language,
reading and bobbing.

The language pulses for her
and bobbing places
the Word in the Place
wherever she is.
Wherever she is, she can
take that book from
her bag, extract those
words from the Book, find
order and rhythm
within the chaos surrounding her.

Now she puts the book down
and begins to rub her hands together,
rubbing and bobbing,
rubbing the words into her skin,
the friction of her palms
warming the words,
making it easier to absorb them
into her blood.

Ah, to have one book!
To be able to bob with the rhythm
and order of symbols,
to be satisfied by symbols,
to sing in the cave of language,

bobbing and reading and
rubbing two words together
in just the right way
to produce the spark of god.

This is the book we all must write,
each in our daily prayer,
whatever the form, whatever the rhythm,
we bob and read and rub and write
on the verge of revelation.

Littering

A single shoe punctuating the double yellow line
  of a country road is obviously a mistake,
  something held in a dog's mouth, perhaps,
  an hour or two ago, until at this very spot
  a rabbit decided to hop into the underbrush,
  causing the jaw momentarily to slacken.

A tin can by the side of the road, or even two or three,
  must have been snipped from a fender
  in this quiet place by the newly married,
  finally weary of the proclaiming clatter.

Let us declare right now that anything tossed
  from a window by someone four or younger
  is most likely just an experiment in wind
  currents or emerging independence and
  shouldn't be held against the young Newton.
  That probably accounts for any number of
  rattles, toys, and dissertation pages
  strewn along the highway margins.

Even that bag of festering garbage stinking up
  the joint for miles around might have fallen
  off the tailgate of a pickup on the lurch of takeoff,
  leaving its former owner scratching his head
  later at the dump.

And I am ready to posit a story of woe or personal tragedy
  for the unfortunate soul who last night blindly
  flung what became those shards of amber glass
  on my front lawn this morning, several pieces
  strung together by a red and white label and glue.

I can scarcely believe there is anyone among us
who sees a stand of ferns at the edge of the road,
surrounded by their aureole of sand,
and finds absolutely no connection with himself.

On Hearing That Someone Bought a House on Nantucket Island for 7.9 Million Dollars and Then Razed It to Build One They Liked Better

I am a fine black ant. I clean my fine antennae:
first the right, then the left. I comb the surface
of your sink for crumbs, settle for a spot of wine.
I never stop working; I take whatever I need.

I am a fine young skunk, the one whose scent your dog
brought in last week and carried from room to room.
I was that thump under your new car last night,
my intestines you saw today, toothpaste from a tube.

I am a fine mosquito. My life is short
but oh so rich. Your sweat attracts me to your fine skin.
I sample the bouquet of your blood. You slap me,
and the stain on your hand comes off completely.

At night I listen to the fog swallow your dark house
and wonder what in the world will stop you.

Therapy

God's psychiatrist was tired;
the litany of sins he listened to every week
seemed infinite: war, famine,
injustice, cruelty, tortures of all kinds:
a slow starvation; the rape of a child;
a holocaust for profit. Some
made his skin crawl; some made him weep.
Each time the psychiatrist swore
he wouldn't go back.

Through it all God just talked. He
lay back on the couch with his fingers
locked gently behind his head.
He just wanted to talk, he said,
just needed to get it all off his chest.
"I can't tell you how good this is,"
he exclaimed one week.
"I should be paying you more."
His smile was so bright, the psychiatrist
had to avert his eyes.

Icara

—for Marian

Oh, Steve
she said
I don't think I can do it.

She paced the top of the cliff,
a loose contraption of feathers and bamboo and wax
hung from her shoulders, her hands gripping
the leather thongs inside the frame;
the wind was steady at fifteen knots,
the water far below a shimmering plain.

They've made me doubt myself,
just a few words have thrown me off
she said
and kicked a stone over the side.
It clattered down and down the face,
the sound diminishing by steps
until the air absorbed it.

Just now as I walked past them at the docks,
they stood there and laughed,
called me a silly *girl* bound
on bending the rules of the world
and toasted each other with a sneer.
They said I lacked hubris.
Hubris! As if it were a talisman
to ward off gravity, a shiny word
that only men can use. As if they knew
what binds the universe, as if they knew.

They see only the landscape of disaster
handed down from their fathers,
tales of woe, and loss, and ruin,
all the good things to worry about
while time spins out in a tangled thread
from day to day.

She closed her eyes and sighed:
the air she exhaled became a small bird
whose flight away from us formed a string
of graceful undulations.

Spirit sustained me when I *was* a girl,
before the ignorant armies wore me down.
Once, at my grandparents' house
I decided to roll home,
do somersaults all the way down the hill to my house.
My grandfather said it would get too dark, or
I would lose my way, or I was too small. But
my grandmother reached for a bowl on the shelf,
removed a smooth green stone and a feather,
the earth and air. She tucked them in my pocket—
I have them still—
and wished me luck.

I tucked my head between my knees,
grabbed my shins and tumbled forward,
bumping along slowly at first, awkwardly,
relying on inner sight to guide me. Soon,
I was rolling smoothly over and
over myself, dizzyingly fast yet clear
inside. That day I was just one blur
of revolutions.

She grew quiet on the cliff;
eyes closed, she seemed to turn inside once more,

inhaling light from the memory, perhaps,
from her grandmother, or *her* grandmother before her.
Then something in the way she raised her chin and
curved her back told me she could picture taking off.
In a long pause way up high on the cliff
there was nothing but our breathing and the breeze.
When she opened her eyes
I could see the storm had passed.

Men have the wrong idea about flying
she said, and smiled, shaking her head.
With them it is all ego,
and that's why most will never fly.

Flying should be possible if all the parties agree:
the air, the sea, and gravity.
One doesn't fly over something or through something
but with everything, in balance.
Balance is the key, and harmony,
and breathing, breathing too is very important,
underrated when men speak of flight. Why,
the exchange of air is everything.

Then, with a great flutter of wings and a sharp cry
she was off. She dropped first, and my breath
caught in my throat. I thought of the stone, the men,
pieces of wing and flesh strewn everywhere.
But then she found warm air and soared,
far above the crowd below.
And there was no fear of the wax melting,
the wings separating, her falling into the sea
for she was guided not by the sun
but by the moon, reflecting her own light.

Now, every time I look at the moon
it's still there.

The Tail

After a rich night of dreams
I woke up this morning with a long ponytail.
This is the way it was years ago, yet how could this be?
I stood and peered into the mirror. It was no lie.
Overnight it had returned, neatly braided
and cinched with bright elastics:
green, blue, red.

My wife was delighted and wanted to
unbraid it and make love immediately.
I thought she might have sewn it on
in the night, but her quick tug told me
it had grown from the scalp.

I had been reading about Indians
for the past few weeks, and I knew
the power of language. Lame Deer's words
read carefully enough,
combined with a certain dream,
might produce a little hair.
But this familiar appendage seemed returned,
filaments conducting some message.

I examined the tail of brown and gray
strands. Somewhere, I realized, they've elected
more Republicans. In a small town, someone
just told a musician he needs to get a real job.
Or a woman mouthed off and the billy club came down
again. Across town, perhaps, a CEO dipped his foot
in the pool to see if the temp was just right.
In a jungle or a desert somewhere,
another city kid just crossed himself and kissed his dog tags.

In a minute or two, each strand had a voice,
each strand had weight, and the community of hairs
became a rope that pulled me into their choir.

Saving the World

At the conference
on saving the world,
after the speaker
has outlined
how it is to be done,
in clear, forceful terms,
he asks for questions.

Eight or ten hands go up,
and by the end
of the second question—
not a question, really,
but a five-minute
soapbox—
the activists fight
in sarcastic tones
over who was next
until the great man
has to number them
to keep the peace.

Song of the Canaries

It's dark inside this poem. But come in, welcome.
That light on your helmet will help you, until
your mind adjusts. Look around, if you like,
at our community. Like you we've come inside.
At first we hardly knew where to begin, so we put faith
in inklings, the deeper the better. Soon we
just sat together in a quiet circle. The longer
we breathed, the more layers we peeled off.

Here we share the air. We share the water. We
share the food. Here, have some of my crackers.
We make them here, but the grain comes from outside.
We know the woman who grows it, we know the land.
They taste good, don't they? But of course truth
has many layers.

Some of what we learn comes to us in tiny
fragments, like shards from ancient bowls.
Here, we try to assemble them. We try to remember.
Your light could be the piece we need.
Have you finished those crackers? You must
need water now. Here, I'll pour us each a cupful.
I see it makes you frown. Don't worry,
it comes from quite deep in the ground.

Anyway, if the water is bad, I'll know it before you.
You see, I am one of the canaries here, one of the
sensitives. I am one who goes before. See that little girl
over there, the one with the short blond hair? She's
a canary, too. Last month she ate some Perdue chicken

and her throat swelled shut. Now we don't eat
that kind of chicken. Now when she eats
we say she eats for all of us.

Maybe you heard about the Jacobsen boy
who played tag on the neighbor's lawn in his bare feet.
He couldn't read the tiny yellow signs—now
his fever won't go down. There are more of us than
you might think. Friends of yours, with mysterious
headaches? A relative who had a tumor? A child
down the street the symptom men just can't cure?

It gets more obvious, doesn't it. It's true: now
all day long we say of course, of course.

Last Summer

In the last summer of America, everyone
ate cheeseburgers, smiling as the grease ran down
their chins and had to be dammed with a wrist.
Everyone ate ice cream and talked about
how hot it was, how hot it would be tomorrow,
and how 'bout those Dodgers, those Yankees, those Mets.

In the last summer of America, everyone
mowed their lawns to stubble, kept watering
at night or on alternate weekdays,
had cookouts with Joe from the office,
had tag sales where glass bottles and Tom Swift books
traded cellars and attics, and no one could get
enough lemonade.

In the last summer of America, everyone
made one last trip to Disney World, to ride inside
Space Mountain over and over, to see
Mike Fink's Keelboat Ride where the water
splashed over the boat right into your face,
where the line to the Pepsi pavilion snaked
in and out of the chutes and fences strung
along the tarmac, and senior citizens keeled
over like dogs left in the car.

In that last summer of America, fireworks
burst like spiders and rained their red and blue
legs onto the crowd below, happy, so happy,
to look up at the sky from their soft blankets
on the warm, dark earth.

5.

Poet Town

When we were kids, we were adorable,
auditioning sounds from our strollers,
sounds like *peach*, and *pollywog*, and *zanzibar*
as our mothers trotted behind us down Calliope Road.
Later, we rode to practice in the neighbor's van,
the one with the bumpersticker that said
"I Brake for Fire and Ice."

We of course excelled in the improvisation called
school. Our teacher in sixth grade, after
twenty-two years used to this sort of thing,
matched us in groups by poetic predilection:
"Free-versers over there, please, by the window.
New formalists at the file cabinets. Naturists out
on the playground, and no picking *anything* today."

Words were toys that never wore out. We stacked blocks
of them, or strung them in trains, went fishing with them
in the stream of activities that carried off our childhoods.
We flirted with the powerful ones, the ones
that could stop an adult conversation with just one syllable.
But our parents never washed our mouths out with soap,
for they knew from their own experience in our town
that words put on a list might as well be
passed out like gum.

You might think we lived too much in our heads
but I remember stumbling up Dante's Hill
like a tired cliché at the end of a day of throwing
heavy words like *love* and *job* and *destiny* back and forth,
their consonants snapping in our leather gloves.
On hot summer days I'd swim in cool words
until my lips turned blue.

It's true there is pettiness even among poets,
and its snout appeared in the local high school
when eighty-seven of us wanted to be editor
of the school's literary magazine, *The Terza Rima*,
even with the school rule made generations ago
that the editor could not select her own work.
As in all towns there were matters of class and race,
but I like to think they mattered less, that
art subdued them with its love of differences.

Some people think a town couldn't run
with all of its occupations filled by poets,
but we've had plenty of doctors and actuaries
and fishermen and farmers to go around.
A town built on the play of language moves slower than the rest,
and the bottom line is the fourteenth, in a sonnet,
but the tomatoes ripen, the clouds pass overhead,
and people still die when their time has come.

Occasionally at a town council meeting one of the members
will stare off into space for a while and then perhaps
pull out a pad and pencil and jot something down,
and if someone spots a bluebird returning in mid-March
to the box on the pole on the Town Hall lawn, well,
the members know when to adjourn.